STARTING YOUR
CYBER SECURITY
CAREER

BUILDING A SUCCESSFUL CAREER IN CYBER SECURITY

LUCIANO FERRARI, CISSP, CISM, CRISC, C|CISO

TABLE OF CONTENTS

	Introduction	2
1	Understanding Cyber Security	5
2	Types of Cyber Security Jobs	10
3	Salary Expectations	17
4	Educational Pathways	22
5	Certifications	27
6	Skills and Competencies	34
7	Gaining Experience	41
8	Job Search and Application Process	48
9	Career Advancement	55
10	Resources and Tools	61

INTRODUCTION

Welcome to "Starting Your Cyber Security Career: A Comprehensive Guide." My name is Luciano Ferrari, Founder and CEO of LufSec, where we specialize in providing top-notch cyber security consulting and training. As someone passionate about the field, I've created this guide to help you embark on a fulfilling and dynamic career in cyber security.

IMPORTANCE OF CYBER SECURITY IN TODAY'S WORLD

In our increasingly digital world, cyber security has become a critical field. Organizations and individuals face numerous cyber threats daily that can compromise sensitive data, disrupt operations, and cause significant financial loss. The need for skilled cyber security professionals, from small businesses to large corporations and government agencies, has never been greater. By choosing a career in this field, you will play a vital role in protecting valuable digital assets and ensuring the safety and integrity of our interconnected systems.

www.lufsec.com

OVERVIEW OF THE CYBER SECURITY CAREER PATH

The path to a successful career in cyber security is diverse and filled with opportunities. Whether you're interested in protecting networks, analyzing threats, or responding to incidents, you have a role. This guide will provide you with a comprehensive overview of the various job roles within cyber security, the skills and certifications you'll need, and practical steps to help you start and advance your career.

HOW TO USE THIS GUIDE

This eBook is a practical resource to refer to at every stage of your cyber security career journey. Each chapter covers a crucial aspect of the field, from understanding basic concepts to landing your first job and beyond. Here's how you can make the most of this guide:

- **Read Sequentially**: It's best to read the chapters in order if you're starting from scratch. Each section builds on the previous one, providing a logical progression from foundational knowledge to advanced career strategies.

- **Refer to Specific Sections**: Feel free to jump to the relevant chapter if you have questions or need guidance on a particular topic. The table of contents and chapter summaries will help you navigate the book efficiently.

www.lufsec.com

- **Take Notes and Reflect**: As you read, take notes on key points and reflect on how the information applies to your personal career goals. This will help you internalize the knowledge and develop a clear action plan.

- **Utilize the Resources**: Each chapter includes recommendations for further reading, online courses, and practical tools. Use these resources to deepen your understanding and enhance your skills.

OUR MISSION AT LUFSEC

At LufSec, we aim to empower individuals with the knowledge and skills to excel in cyber security. Education and consulting are key to building a safer digital world. Through our consulting services and training courses, we aim to provide practical, hands-on support that prepares you for real-world challenges.

Whether you're a beginner or an experienced professional looking to upskill, we have the resources to support your journey.

Thank you for choosing this guide as your companion when starting a cybersecurity career. I'm excited to be a part of your journey and look forward to seeing you succeed in this dynamic and rewarding field.

www.lufsec.com

CHAPTER 1: UNDERSTANDING CYBERSECURITY

INTRODUCTION TO CYBERSECURITY

Cyber security, also known as information security, protects systems, networks, and programs from digital attacks. These attacks typically target sensitive information, extort money from users, or interrupt normal business processes.

In today's digital age, cyber security is crucial because it helps protect an organization's data and ensures its confidentiality, integrity, and availability. Cyber security measures are designed to combat threats compromising systems and data safety.

www.lufsec.com

KEY CONCEPTS AND TERMINOLOGY

Before diving into the specifics of a cyber security career, it's essential to understand some fundamental concepts and terminology:

- Threat: Any circumstance or event with the potential to cause harm to an information system.
- Vulnerability: A weakness in a system or its design that a threat could exploit.
- Risk: The potential for an asset's loss, damage, or destruction due to a threat exploiting a vulnerability.
- Attack: An attempt to exploit a vulnerability for unauthorized access or damage.
- Incident: A security event that compromises an information asset's integrity, confidentiality, or availability.

OVERVIEW OF CYBER THREATS AND VULNERABILITIES

Cyber threats and vulnerabilities constantly evolve; understanding them is critical for any cybersecurity professional. Here are some of the most common types of threats and vulnerabilities:

1. Malware
Malware, short for malicious software, includes viruses, worms, trojans, ransomware, spyware, adware, and other harmful programs. Malware can disrupt operations, steal sensitive information, or gain unauthorized access to systems.

www.lufsec.com

2. Phishing

Phishing attacks involve tricking individuals into providing sensitive information, such as usernames, passwords, and credit card details, by pretending to be trustworthy. This is typically done via email or other forms of electronic communication.

3. Man-in-the-Middle (MitM) Attacks

MitM attacks occur when an attacker intercepts and alters communication between two parties without their knowledge. This can allow the attacker to steal information or inject malicious content into the communication.

4. Denial-of-Service (DoS) and Distributed Denial-of-Service (DDoS) Attacks

DoS attacks overwhelm a machine or network resource with internet traffic, making it unavailable to its intended users. They are launched from multiple compromised devices, making them harder to defend against.

5. SQL Injection

SQL injection attacks involve inserting malicious SQL code into a query to manipulate a database. This can lead to unauthorized viewing, modification, or deletion of database data.

6. Zero-Day Exploits

Zero-day exploits target vulnerabilities in software that are unknown to the software vendor. Attackers exploit these vulnerabilities before patching them, making them particularly dangerous.

www.lufsec.com

7. Advanced Persistent Threats (APTs)

APTs are prolonged and targeted cyber attacks in which an intruder gains access to a network and remains undetected for an extended period. The goal is often to steal data rather than to cause damage.

Protecting Against Cyber Threats

To protect against these threats, cyber security professionals employ a range of strategies and tools, including:

- **Firewalls:** Act as a barrier between a trusted internal network and untrusted external networks, controlling incoming and outgoing network traffic.
- **Intrusion Detection Systems (IDS) and Intrusion Prevention Systems (IPS)**: Monitor network traffic for suspicious activity and take action to prevent or mitigate threats.
- **Encryption**: Converts unreadable data into a secure format without the proper decryption key, protecting sensitive information from unauthorized access.
- **Antivirus and Anti-Malware Software**: Detect and remove malicious software from computers and networks.
- **Security Information and Event Management (SIEM)**: Aggregates and analyzes activity from multiple resources across an IT infrastructure to detect and respond to potential security threats.
- **Patch Management**: Ensures software updates and patches are applied promptly to fix vulnerabilities.

- **User Education and Awareness:** Training users to recognize and respond to cyber threats like phishing emails can significantly reduce the risk of successful attacks.

Understanding these fundamental concepts and the nature of cyber threats will better equip you to start your journey in cyber security.

The next chapter will delve into the various types of cyber security jobs available, providing insights into the roles and responsibilities you can expect in this exciting career.

CHAPTER 2: TYPES OF CYBER SECURITY JOBS

Cybersecurity offers various job roles with unique responsibilities and skill requirements. Understanding these roles will help you identify the career path that best aligns with your interests and strengths.

SECURITY ANALYST

Responsibilities:

- Monitor networks and systems for security breaches.
- Investigate and respond to security incidents.
- Implement and maintain security measures and tools.
- Conduct vulnerability assessments and penetration testing.
- Prepare reports and documentation on security status and incidents.

Skills Required:

- Strong analytical and problem-solving skills.
- Knowledge of networking and operating systems.
- Familiarity with security tools and technologies (e.g., SIEM, IDS/IPS).
- Understanding of threat modeling and risk assessment techniques.

Typical Salary:

- Entry-Level: $50,000 - $70,000
- Mid-Level: $70,000 - $90,000
- Senior-Level: $90,000 - $120,000

SECURITY ENGINEER
Responsibilities:

- Design and implement secure network solutions.
- Develop and enforce security policies and procedures.
- Maintain and update security systems, such as firewalls and intrusion detection systems.
- Perform regular security audits and assessments.
- Collaborate with IT and development teams to secure applications and infrastructure.

Skills Required:

- Strong technical background in networking and system administration.
- Experience with security technologies (e.g., firewalls, VPNs, IDS/IPS).

www.lufsec.com

- Knowledge of scripting and automation tools.
- Understanding of secure coding practices and software development life cycle (SDLC).

Typical Salary:

- Entry-Level: $70,000 - $90,000
- Mid-Level: $90,000 - $110,000
- Senior-Level: $110,000 - $140,000

SECURITY ARCHITECT
Responsibilities:

- Develop and design security architecture for systems and networks.
- Ensure compliance with security standards and best practices.
- Assess and mitigate risks associated with new and existing systems.
- Create and maintain security policies, procedures, and guidelines.
- Provide strategic guidance on security initiatives and projects.

Skills Required:

- Extensive knowledge of security principles and frameworks.
- Experience in designing and implementing security solutions.
- Strong understanding of enterprise architecture and cloud security.

www.lufsec.com

- Ability to communicate security concepts to technical and non-technical stakeholders.

Typical Salary:

- Entry-Level: $90,000 - $110,000
- Mid-Level: $110,000 - $140,000
- Senior-Level: $140,000 - $180,000

PENETRATION TESTER (ETHICAL HACKER)
Responsibilities:

- Conduct simulated attacks on systems and networks to identify vulnerabilities.
- Develop and execute penetration testing plans and methodologies.
- Report findings and provide recommendations for remediation.
- Stay updated on the latest security threats and techniques.
- Collaborate with security teams to improve defenses.

Skills Required:

- Proficiency in various penetration testing tools and techniques.
- Strong understanding of networking, operating systems, and web applications.
- Knowledge of scripting languages (e.g., Python, Bash).
- Ability to think like an attacker and identify creative exploitation methods.

Typical Salary:

- Entry-Level: $70,000 - $90,000
- Mid-Level: $90,000 - $120,000
- Senior-Level: $120,000 - $150,000

INCIDENT RESPONDER

Responsibilities:

- Investigate and respond to security incidents and breaches.
- Perform forensic analysis to determine the cause and extent of incidents.
- Develop and implement incident response plans and procedures.
- Coordinate with other teams and stakeholders during incidents.
- Document incidents and lessons learned to improve future response efforts.

Skills Required:

- Strong analytical and investigative skills.
- Experience with forensic tools and techniques.
- Knowledge of incident response frameworks and best practices.
- Ability to remain calm and effective under pressure.

Typical Salary:

- Entry-Level: $60,000 - $80,000
- Mid-Level: $80,000 - $100,000

www.lufsec.com

- Senior-Level: $100,000 - $130,000

SECURITY CONSULTANT
Responsibilities:

- Assess clients' security needs and provide expert advice.
- Conduct security assessments and audits.
- Develop and recommend security strategies and solutions.
- Assist clients with compliance and regulatory requirements.
- Provide training and awareness programs for clients.

Skills Required:

- Strong knowledge of security standards and best practices.
- Experience with risk assessment and management.
- Excellent communication and presentation skills.
- Ability to tailor solutions to clients' specific needs.

Typical Salary:

Entry-Level: $70,000 - $90,000
Mid-Level: $90,000 - $120,000
Senior-Level: $120,000 - $150,000

www.lufsec.com

CHIEF INFORMATION SECURITY OFFICER (CISO)
Responsibilities:

- Develop and implement the organization's security strategy.
- Oversee the security operations and teams.
- Ensure compliance with security regulations and standards.
- Communicate security risks and strategies to executive leadership.
- Lead incident response efforts and manage security budgets.

Skills Required:

- Extensive experience in security management and leadership.
- Strong understanding of regulatory and compliance requirements.
- Excellent strategic planning and communication skills.
- Ability to influence and drive security initiatives at the executive level.

Typical Salary:
-
- Entry-Level: $120,000 - $150,000
- Mid-Level: $150,000 - $200,000

Senior-Level: $200,000 - $250,000+

www.lufsec.com

Other Roles (e.g., Cryptographer, Forensic Expert)

CRIPTOGRAPHER

- **Responsibilities:** Design and implement cryptographic algorithms and systems.
- **Skills Required**: Strong background in mathematics and cryptography.
- **Typical Salary**: $90,000 - $140,000

FORENSIC EXPERT

- **Responsibilities**: Conduct digital forensic investigations to uncover evidence of cyber crimes.
- **Skills Required**: Proficiency in forensic tools and techniques and attention to detail.
- **Typical Salary**: $70,000 - $110,000

This chapter has provided an overview of various job roles within the field of cyber security. Each role offers unique challenges and opportunities, and understanding these can help you choose a career path that aligns with your interests and strengths. In the next chapter, we will explore the salary expectations for different cybersecurity jobs and the factors that can influence earnings in this field.

www.lufsec.com

CHAPTER 3: SALARY EXPECTATIONS

Understanding salary expectations is crucial as you plan your cyber security career. This field's salary can vary widely based on job role, experience, education, location, and certifications. This chapter overviews typical salaries for cyber security jobs and the factors influencing these earnings.

Entry-Level Salaries

For those just starting in cyber security, entry-level positions offer competitive salaries, reflecting the high demand for skilled professionals in this field. Here are typical salary ranges for some entry-level roles:

- **Security Analyst**: $50,000 - $70,000
- **Penetration Tester**: $70,000 - $90,000
- **Incident Responder**: $60,000 - $80,000
- **Security Engineer**: $70,000 - $90,000

www.lufsec.com

Mid-Level Salaries

With a few years of experience and additional skills or certifications, you can expect to move into mid-level positions with higher pay. Mid-level roles often involve more responsibility and expertise:

- **Security Analyst**: $70,000 - $90,000
- **Penetration Tester**: $90,000 - $120,000
- **Incident Responder**: $80,000 - $100,000
- **Security Engineer**: $90,000 - $110,000

Senior-Level Salaries

Senior-level positions typically require significant experience and advanced certifications and offer substantial salaries. These roles often involve leadership responsibilities and strategic decision-making:

- **Security Architect**: $140,000 - $180,000
- **Chief Information Security Officer (CISO)**: $200,000 - $250,000+
- **Senior Security Consultant**: $120,000 - $150,000
- **Lead Penetration Tester**: $120,000 - $150,000

FACTORS AFFECTING SALARY

1. Location

Salaries can vary significantly based on geographic location. For example, cyber security professionals in major tech hubs like San Francisco, New York, and Washington D.C. tend to earn higher salaries due to the higher cost of living and higher demand for skilled workers.

2. Experience

Experience is a significant determinant of salary. As you gain more experience in the field, you can expect to see substantial increases in your earnings. Senior-level positions that require extensive experience often come with high salaries.

3. Education

Having a relevant degree can impact your starting salary and career progression. Advanced degrees, such as a Master's in Cyber Security, can lead to higher wages and more advanced job opportunities.

4. Certifications

Certifications play a significant role in determining salaries in cyber security. Employers highly value certifications such as CISSP, CEH, CISM, and others and can significantly boost your earning potential.

www.lufsec.com

5. Industry

The industry you work in can also affect your salary. Specific industries, such as finance, healthcare, and defense, may offer higher wages due to the critical nature of the data they handle and the stringent security requirements.

Sample Salary Data

Here's a snapshot of average salaries for various cybersecurity roles based on industry reports and surveys:

Job Role	Entry-Level Salary	Mid-Level Salary	Senior-Level Salary
Security Analyst	$50,000 - $70,000	$70,000 - $90,000	$90,000 - $120,000
Security Engineer	$70,000 - $90,000	$90,000 - $110,000	$110,000 - $140,000
Security Architect	$90,000 - $110,000	$110,000 - $140,000	$140,000 - $180,000
Penetration Tester	$70,000 - $90,000	$90,000 - $120,000	$120,000 - $150,000
Incident Responder	$60,000 - $80,000	$80,000 - $100,000	$100,000 - $130,000
Security Consultant	$70,000 - $90,000	$90,000 - $120,000	$120,000 - $150,000
CISO	$120,000 - $150,000	$150,000 - $200,000	$200,000 - $250,000+

Conclusion

Salaries in cyber security are generally high compared to many other fields, reflecting the critical importance and high demand for skilled professionals. By understanding the factors influencing salaries, you can better plan your career path and make informed decisions about education, certifications, and job opportunities.

The next chapter will explore the educational pathways available to aspiring cybersecurity professionals, including formal education, self-learning, and specialized training programs.

CHAPTER 4: EDUCATIONAL PATHWAYS

A solid educational foundation is essential for a successful career in cyber security. Various pathways exist to gain the necessary knowledge and skills, including formal education, self-learning, and specialized training programs. This chapter explores these options and provides recommendations to help you choose the best path for your career goals.

FORMAT EDUCATION

1. Degree Programs

Pursuing a degree in cyber security, computer science, or a related field is a common and effective way to enter the cyber security field. Degree programs offer a structured curriculum that covers essential topics and provides a comprehensive understanding of the field.

www.lufsec.com

- **Associate Degree**: Typically a two-year program that provides foundational knowledge in cyber security and IT. It's a good starting point for entry-level positions.
- **Bachelor's Degree**: A four-year program that offers in-depth study of cyber security principles, programming, networking, and more. A bachelor's degree is often required for mid-level positions and can significantly enhance career prospects.
- **Master's Degree**: Advanced study in cyber security or a related field, focusing on specialized topics and research. A master's degree can open doors to senior-level positions and specialized roles.

Recommended Institutions and Programs:

- **University of Maryland University College (UMUC)**: Offers a well-regarded Bachelor's and Master's in Cyber Security.
- **Stanford University**: Provides advanced courses and degrees in cyber security through its Cyber Security Program.
- **Massachusetts Institute of Technology (MIT)**: Known for its cutting-edge research and programs in computer science and cyber security.

2. Online Degree Programs

Online degree programs offer flexibility and convenience. They allow you to study at your own pace while balancing other commitments. Many reputable institutions now offer online degrees in cyber security.

- **Western Governors University (WGU)**: Offers an online Bachelor's and Master's in Cyber Security.
- **Southern New Hampshire University (SNHU)**: Provides various online degrees in information technology and cyber security.
- **Drexel University**: Offers online programs in computing and security technology.

Self-Learning and Online Courses

Self-learning through online courses is a cost-effective and flexible way to gain cybersecurity knowledge. Many platforms offer beginner to advanced-level courses, allowing you to learn at your own pace.

Recommended Online Learning Platforms:

- **Coursera**: Offers courses and specializations in cyber security from top universities and organizations, such as the University of London and IBM.
- **edX**: Provides courses from institutions like Harvard University and MIT, covering various cybersecurity topics.
- **Udemy**: Features many cyber security courses, including ethical hacking, penetration testing, and more.
- **Cybrary**: A platform dedicated to cyber security training with courses for all skill levels.
- **LufSec**: Offers a variety of cyber security courses and training programs designed to equip you with practical, hands-on skills.

www.lufsec.com

Bootcamps and Workshops

Cyber security bootcamps and workshops offer intensive, hands-on training over a short period. These programs equip you with practical skills and knowledge, often culminating in a project or certification.

Recommended Bootcamps:

- **SANS Institute**: Known for its rigorous training programs and certifications in cyber security.
- **Cybrary Bootcamps**: Provides various bootcamps focused on specific cyber security skills and certifications.
- **Springboard Cyber Security Bootcamp**: Offers a comprehensive curriculum with one-on-one mentorship.

Certifications

Certifications are highly valued in cybersecurity and can significantly enhance your career prospects. They demonstrate your expertise and commitment to the field.

Popular Certifications:

- **CompTIA Security+**: An entry-level certification covering foundational security concepts.
- **Certified Information Systems Security Professional (CISSP)**: An advanced certification for experienced professionals covering various security topics.

www.lufsec.com

- **Certified Ethical Hacker (CEH):** Focuses on ethical hacking techniques and tools.
- **Certified Information Security Manager (CISM):** Emphasizes management and governance of information security programs.
- **Certified Information Systems Auditor (CISA):** Focuses on auditing, control, and assurance.

Study Tips and Resources

1. Create a Study Plan

You can outline your goals and set a study schedule. Break down the material into manageable sections. Allocate time for regular review and practice.

2. Utilize Multiple Resources

Combine textbooks, online courses, and practical labs. Join study groups and online forums for support and collaboration.
Use practice exams and quizzes to test your knowledge.

3. Stay Current

- Follow industry news and updates to stay informed about emerging threats and trends.
- Participate in webinars, workshops, and conferences.
- Engage with the cyber security community through forums and social media.

Recommended Study Materials

Books:
- "The Web Application Hacker's Handbook" by Dafydd Stuttard and Marcus Pinto: An excellent resource for learning about web application security.
- "Hacking: The Art of Exploitation" by Jon Erickson: Provides a deep dive into hacking techniques and methodologies.
- "Metasploit: The Penetration Tester's Guide" by David Kennedy, Jim O'Gorman, Devon Kearns, and Mati Aharoni: Covers practical penetration testing using the Metasploit framework.

Websites and Forums:
- Reddit (r/netsec): A community for discussing information security news and topics.
- Stack Exchange (Information Security): A Q&A site for security professionals and enthusiasts.
- OWASP (Open Web Application Security Project): Provides resources and tools for web application security.

Conclusion

Choosing the right educational pathway is crucial for building a successful career in cyber security. Whether you opt for a formal degree, self-learning, or specialized training programs, there are ample opportunities to gain the knowledge and skills needed to thrive in this field. In the next chapter, we will explore the importance of certifications and how to select the right ones to enhance your career prospects.

www.lufsec.com

CHAPTER 5: CERTIFICATIONS

Certifications are a crucial component of a cyber security career. They validate your skills, knowledge, and commitment to the field, making you a more attractive candidate to employers. This chapter will cover the importance of certifications, provide an overview of popular certifications, and offer tips on choosing the right ones for your career goals.

IMPORTANCE OF CERTIFICATIONS

1. Industry Recognition

- Certifications are widely recognized in the industry and often serve as a benchmark for assessing a candidate's qualifications.
- They demonstrate your dedication to continuous learning and professional development.

www.lufsec.com

2. Enhanced Career Prospects
- Relevant certifications can significantly improve your job prospects and open doors to advanced positions.
- Many employers require specific certifications for certain roles, making them essential for career advancement.

3. Increased Earning Potential
- Certifications can lead to higher salaries. Professionals with certifications often earn more than their non-certified counterparts.
- Certain certifications, especially advanced ones, are associated with substantial salary increases.

OVERVIEW OF POPULAR CERTIFICATIONS

1. CompTIA Security+

- **Description:** An entry-level certification covering fundamental security concepts, tools, and procedures.
- **Topics Covered:** Network security, compliance and operational security, threats and vulnerabilities, application and data security, and more.
- **Who Should Pursue:** Ideal for beginners looking to establish a foundation in cyber security.
- **Prerequisites:** None, but basic IT knowledge is recommended.
- **Exam Details:** Multiple-choice and performance-based questions.
- **Study Resources:** Official CompTIA study guides, online courses (LufSec.com, Udemy), and practice exams.

www.lufsec.com

2. Certified Information Systems Security Professional (CISSP)

- **Description:** An advanced certification for experienced professionals covering various security topics.
- **Topics Covered**: Security and risk management, asset security, security architecture and engineering, communication and network security, and more.
- **Who Should Pursue**: Professionals with at least five years of experience in information security.
- **Prerequisites**: Five years of cumulative, paid work experience in two or more of the eight CISSP domains.
- **Exam Details**: Multiple-choice and advanced innovative questions.
- **Study Resources**: Official CISSP study guide, online courses (LufSec.com, Coursera), practice exams.

3. Certified Ethical Hacker (CEH)

- **Description**: Focuses on ethical hacking techniques and tools.
- **Topics Covered**: Footprinting and reconnaissance, scanning networks, enumeration, system hacking, malware threats, social engineering, and more.
- **Who Should Pursue**: Individuals interested in penetration testing and ethical hacking.
- **Prerequisites**: Two years of work experience in information security (waived if attending official EC-Council training).

- **Exam Details:** Multiple-choice questions.
- **Study Resources**: Official CEH study guide, online courses (LufSec.com, Cybrary), practice exams.

4. Certified Information Security Manager (CISM)

- **Description**: Emphasizes management and governance of information security programs.
- **Topics Covered**: Information security governance, risk management, information security program development and management, incident management.
- **Who Should Pursue**: Information security managers and those with information security management responsibilities.
- **Prerequisites**: Five years of work experience in information security management.
- **Exam Details**: Multiple-choice questions.
- **Study Resources**: Official ISACA study guide, online courses (LufSec.com, edX), practice exams.

5. Certified Information Systems Auditor (CISA)

- **Description**: Focuses on auditing, control, and assurance.
- **Topics Covered**: Information system auditing process, governance and management of IT, information systems acquisition, development and implementation, information systems operations and business resilience, and protection of information assets.

- **Who Should Pursue:** IT auditors, audit managers, consultants.
- **Prerequisites**: Five years of experience in information systems auditing, control, or security.
- **Exam Details**: Multiple-choice questions.
- **Study Resources**: Official ISACA study guide, online courses (LufSec.com, Coursera), practice exams.

HOW TO CHOOSE THE RIGHT CERTIFICATION

1. Assess Your Career Goals
- Determine the specific area of cyber security you are interested in (e.g., network security, ethical hacking, management).
- Identify the certifications that align with your career aspirations and your desired job roles.

2. Evaluate Prerequisites
- Review the prerequisites for each certification to ensure you meet the experience and education requirements.
- If you are new to the field, consider starting with entry-level certifications and progressing to more advanced certifications as you gain experience.

3. Research Industry Requirements

- Look at job postings in your desired field to see which certifications employers most commonly require or prefer.
- Consult with industry professionals and mentors for their recommendations on valuable certifications.

www.lufsec.com

4. Consider Cost and Time Investment

- Evaluate the cost of certification exams and preparation materials.
- Consider the time required to study for and obtain each certification, balancing it with your other commitments.

5. Leverage Study Resources

- Utilize various study resources, such as books, online courses, and practice exams.
- Engage in study groups and online forums to collaborate with others and gain additional insights.

STUDY TIPS FOR CERTIFICATION EXAMS

1. Create a Study Schedule
- Set a realistic study schedule that allows you to cover all the exam topics thoroughly.
- You can schedule regular review and practice tests to reinforce your knowledge.

2. Use Multiple Study Resources
- Combine textbooks, online courses, and practical labs to understand the material better.
- You can take advantage of official study guides and materials provided by certification bodies.

www.lufsec.com

3. Practice with Exam Simulators
- You can use practice exams and exam simulators to familiarize yourself with the format and types of questions you will encounter. Many exam simulators are available at LufSec.com/products.
- Review your answers and understand the rationale behind correct and incorrect responses.

4. Stay Updated
- Keep up with the latest cyber security developments and trends to ensure your knowledge is current.
- Follow industry news, join professional organizations, and participate in relevant webinars and workshops.

Conclusion

Certifications are a vital part of a successful cybersecurity career. They not only validate your skills and knowledge but also enhance your job prospects and earning potential. By carefully selecting the right certifications and dedicating time to study and preparation, you can achieve significant milestones in your career. In the next chapter, we will explore the essential skills and competencies needed for a thriving career in cyber security.

www.lufsec.com

CHAPTER 6: SKILLS AND COMPETENCIES

A successful career in cyber security requires a diverse set of skills and competencies. These include technical abilities, analytical thinking, problem-solving capabilities, and essential soft skills. This chapter will outline the key skills and competencies you need to thrive in cybersecurity and provide tips on developing them.

TECHNICAL SKILLS

1. Networking
   - **Understanding Network Protocols**: Knowledge of TCP/IP, DNS, HTTP/HTTPS, and other protocols is fundamental.
   - **Network Configuration**: Ability to configure and manage routers, switches, and firewalls.
   - **Network Security**: Skills in securing networks, including implementing VLANs, VPNs, and intrusion detection/prevention systems (IDS/IPS).

2. System Administration

- **Operating Systems:** Proficiency in administering and securing various operating systems, such as Windows, Linux, and macOS.
- **Server Management**: Experience with managing servers, including patch management, user access control, and system monitoring.
- **Virtualization and Cloud Computing**: Knowledge of virtual machines and cloud platforms (e.g., AWS, Azure, Google Cloud).

3. Programming and Scripting

- **Languages**: Proficiency in Python, JavaScript, PowerShell, and Bash.
- **Automation**: Ability to write scripts to automate repetitive tasks and enhance security measures.
- **Secure Coding**: Understanding of secure coding practices to prevent vulnerabilities in software.

4. Cyber Security Tools and Technologies

- **Security Information and Event Management (SIEM)**: Experience with tools like Splunk, QRadar, and ArcSight for monitoring and analyzing security events.
- **Penetration Testing Tools**: Proficiency with tools such as Metasploit, Nmap, Burp Suite, and Wireshark.
- **Endpoint Protection**: Knowledge of antivirus, anti-malware, and endpoint detection and response (EDR) tools.

www.lufsec.com

ANALYTICAL AND PROBLEM-SOLVING SKILLS

1. Threat Analysis
- **Identifying Threats:** Ability to identify and assess potential threats and vulnerabilities.
- **Risk Assessment:** Skills in evaluating the likelihood and impact of threats and determining appropriate mitigation strategies.

2. Incident Response
- **Detection and Analysis**: Proficiency in detecting security incidents, analyzing the root cause, and determining the extent of the impact.
- **Containment and Eradication**: Ability to contain and eliminate threats while minimizing damage.
- **Recovery and Lessons Learned**: Skills in restoring systems to normal operations and documenting lessons learned to improve future response efforts.

3. Forensics
- **Data Collection**: Ability to collect and preserve digital evidence forensically soundly.
- **Analysis and Reporting**: Skills in analyzing forensic data and producing comprehensive reports for legal or organizational use.

www.lufsec.com

SOFT SKILLS

1. Communication
- **Clear and Concise Writing:** Ability to document security policies, incident reports, and technical findings effectively.
- **Verbal Communication**: Skills in explaining complex security concepts to non-technical stakeholders.
- **Presentation Skills**: Proficiency in presenting security strategies and findings to management and clients.

2. Critical Thinking
- Analytical Mindset: Ability to analyze complex situations, identify patterns, and make data-driven decisions.
- Problem-Solving: Skills in developing and implementing effective solutions to security challenges.

3. Attention to Detail
- Thoroughness: Ability to pay close attention to details to identify potential security issues and ensure comprehensive coverage of security measures.
- Accuracy: Ensuring accuracy in analysis, reporting, and implementation of security controls.

www.lufsec.com

CONTINUOUS LEARNING AND STAYING UPDATED

1. **Industry News and Trends**
   - **Follow News Outlets:** Stay informed about the latest security threats, breaches, and technological advancements by following reputable news sources.
   - **Join Professional Organizations**: Engage with organizations like ISACA, ISC2, and SANS Institute to access resources, webinars, and networking opportunities.

2. **Training and Certifications**
   - **Pursue Ongoing Education**: Continuously seek opportunities for learning through courses, workshops, and certifications.
   - **Engage in Cyber Security Communities**: Participate in online forums, attend conferences, and join local meetups to share knowledge and stay connected with peers.

3. **Practical Experience**
   - **Home Labs**: Set up a home lab environment to practice and experiment with different tools and techniques.
   - **Capture the Flag (CTF) Competitions**: Participate in CTF competitions to enhance your skills and gain practical experience.
   - **Bug Bounty Programs**: Engage in bug bounty programs to apply your skills in real-world scenarios and earn rewards.

www.lufsec.com

DEVELOPING YOUR SKILLS

1. Create a Learning Plan
- **Set Goals:** Define clear, achievable goals for developing your skills and advancing your career.
- **Identify Resources**: Determine the necessary resources, such as courses, books, and tools.
- **Allocate Time**: Schedule regular study and practice sessions to ensure consistent progress.

2. Hands-On Practice
- **Labs and Simulations**: Use lab environments and simulations to practice your skills in a controlled setting.
- **Real-World Projects**: Work on real-world projects or contribute to open-source security tools to gain practical experience.

3. Seek Feedback and Mentorship
- **Find a Mentor:** Connect with experienced professionals who can provide guidance and feedback.
- **Peer Review**: Participate in peer review sessions to get constructive feedback on your work.

Conclusion

Building a successful career in cyber security requires a combination of technical skills, analytical thinking, problem-solving abilities, and essential soft skills.

www.lufsec.com

You can develop the competencies needed to excel in this dynamic field by continuously learning and staying updated with industry trends. In the next chapter, we will explore ways to gain practical experience, including internships, volunteering, and participating in cybersecurity competitions.

CHAPTER 7: GAINING EXPERIENCE

Practical experience is vital for building a successful career in cyber security. While theoretical knowledge is essential, hands-on experience allows you to apply what you've learned and develop the skills to tackle real-world challenges. This chapter explores various ways to gain practical experience, including internships, volunteering, building a home lab, and participating in cybersecurity competitions.

INTERNSHIPS AND ENTRY-LEVEL JOBS

1. Internships

Internships provide an excellent opportunity to gain hands-on experience while working alongside experienced professionals. They allow you to apply your knowledge in real-world settings and learn from industry experts.

www.lufsec.com

- **Finding Internships:** Look for internships through job boards, company websites, and career fairs. Networking with professionals in the field can also help you discover internship opportunities.
- **What to Expect**: Internships typically involve assisting with day-to-day security tasks, such as monitoring networks, conducting vulnerability assessments, and responding to incidents. You'll gain exposure to various tools and techniques used in the industry.
- **Tips for Success**: Be proactive, ask questions, and seek feedback. Show enthusiasm and a willingness to learn. Treat your internship as a learning experience and an opportunity to make valuable connections.

2. Entry-Level Jobs

Entry-level positions, such as junior security analyst or security technician, provide a gateway to the cybersecurity field. These roles offer practical experience and the chance to develop your skills further.

- **Job Search Strategies**: Use job boards, company websites, and professional networking sites like LinkedIn to find entry-level positions. Tailor your resume and cover letter to highlight your relevant skills and experiences.
- **Interview Preparation**: Prepare for interviews by reviewing common cyber security interview questions and practicing your responses. Be ready to discuss your technical skills, problem-solving abilities, and any hands-on experience you have.

- **On-the-Job Learning:** Take advantage of on-the-job training and mentorship opportunities. Continuously seek ways to improve your skills and contribute to your team's success.

VOLUNTEERING AND FREELANCING

1. Volunteering
Volunteering for non-profit organizations, community groups, or small businesses can provide valuable experience while giving back to the community.

- **Finding Opportunities**: Look for volunteer opportunities through online platforms, local community organizations, and professional associations. Offer your skills to organizations that may need more resources to hire full-time security staff.
- **Benefits**: Volunteering allows you to gain practical experience, build your portfolio, and expand your professional network. It also demonstrates your commitment to the field and your willingness to contribute.

2. Freelancing
Freelancing offers flexibility and the opportunity to work on a variety of projects. It can be a great way to gain experience, especially if you're transitioning into the field or looking to supplement your full-time job.

www.lufsec.com

- **Finding Clients**: Use freelancing platforms like Upwork and Freelancer to find clients looking for cyber security services. Networking and referrals can also help you secure freelance projects.
- **Managing Projects**: Develop strong project management skills to handle multiple clients and deadlines. Communicate clearly with clients to understand their needs and deliver high-quality work.
- **Building a Portfolio**: Use your freelance projects to build a portfolio that showcases your skills and experience. Highlight your achievements and the impact of your work.

BUILDING A HOME LAB

A home lab is an excellent way to gain hands-on experience in a controlled environment. It allows you to experiment with different tools, techniques, and scenarios without the risk of compromising real systems.

1. **Setting Up a Home Lab**
   - **Hardware and Software**: To set up your home lab, use a spare computer, virtual machines, or cloud services. Install various operating systems, security tools, and network devices.
   - **Learning Objectives:** Define your learning objectives and create a plan for what you want to achieve with your home lab. Focus on areas such as network security, penetration testing, malware analysis, and incident response.

www.lufsec.com

- **Resources**: Use online tutorials, forums, and courses to guide your learning. Document your experiments and findings to track your progress.

2. Practical Exercises
- **Network Security**: Set up a small network and practice configuring firewalls, intrusion detection systems, and VPNs. Perform vulnerability assessments and implement security measures.
- **Penetration Testing**: Use tools like Metasploit, Nmap, and Burp Suite to conduct penetration tests on your lab environment. Practice exploiting vulnerabilities and documenting your findings.
- **Malware Analysis**: Analyze malware samples in a controlled environment. Use tools like IDA Pro, OllyDbg, and Wireshark to dissect malware behavior and understand its impact.

PARTICIPATING IN CYBER SECURITY COMPETITIONS

1. Capture the Flag (CTF) Competitions
CTF competitions are popular in the cybersecurity community and provide a fun and challenging way to test your skills. They involve solving security-related challenges to capture "flags" and earn points.

- Types of CTFs: There are two main types of CTFs—jeopardy-style and attack-defense. Jeopardy-style CTFs involve solving a series of challenges, while attack-defense CTFs involve defending your system while attacking others.

www.lufsec.com

- **Finding Competitions**: Look for CTF competitions hosted by universities, professional organizations, and online platforms. Websites like CTFtime.org list upcoming competitions and provide resources for preparation.
- **Preparing for CTFs**: Practice solving CTF challenges on platforms like Hack The Box, TryHackMe, and OverTheWire. Collaborate with others to share knowledge and strategies.

2. Bug Bounty Programs

Bug bounty programs reward individuals for finding and reporting security vulnerabilities in software and websites. They offer a way to gain real-world experience and potentially earn money.

- **Finding Programs**: Join bug bounty platforms like HackerOne, Bugcrowd, and Synack. These platforms connect security researchers with organizations looking to improve their security.
- **Reporting Vulnerabilities**: When reporting vulnerabilities, follow responsible disclosure guidelines. Provide detailed information and proof-of-concept to demonstrate the issue.
- **Building a Reputation**: Consistently finding and reporting valuable vulnerabilities can help you build a reputation in the cyber security community and attract job opportunities.

Conclusion

Gaining practical experience is essential for building a successful career in cyber security. Whether through internships, volunteering, building a home lab, or participating in competitions, hands-on experience allows you to apply your knowledge and develop the skills needed to excel in the field. In the next chapter, we will explore the job search and application process, providing tips on how to create an effective resume, craft a compelling cover letter, and prepare for interviews.

CHAPTER 8: JOB SEARCH AND APPLICATION PROCESS

Navigating the job search and application process can be challenging, especially in a competitive field like cyber security. This chapter provides practical advice on creating an effective resume, crafting a compelling cover letter, and preparing for interviews. Following these guidelines can enhance your chances of landing your desired cybersecurity role.

BUILDING AN EFFECTIVE RESUME

1. **Structure and Format**
   - **Contact Information:** Include your name, phone number, email address, and LinkedIn profile.
   - **Professional Summary**: Write a summary that highlights your essential qualifications and career objectives.

www.lufsec.com

- **Experience**: List your work experience in reverse chronological order. Include job title, company name, location, and dates of employment. Describe your responsibilities and achievements using bullet points.
- **Education**: Include your educational background, listing degrees, institutions, and graduation dates.
- **Certifications**: Highlight relevant certifications, such as CompTIA Security+, CISSP, CEH, and others.
- **Skills**: List technical and soft skills relevant to the job you are applying for.
- **Projects and Achievements**: Include any notable projects, research, publications, or achievements that demonstrate your expertise.

2. Tailoring Your Resume
- **Keywords**: Incorporate keywords from the job description to ensure your resume passes through applicant tracking systems (ATS).
- **Customization**: Tailor your resume for each job application by emphasizing the most relevant experience and skills.
- **Quantify Achievements:** Use metrics and numbers to quantify your achievements (e.g., "Reduced security incidents by 30% through the implementation of a new monitoring system").

3. Design and Layout
- **Clean and Professional:** Use a clean, professional layout with consistent formatting. Avoid using overly decorative fonts or graphics.

- **Readability**: To improve readability, use bullet points and concise language. Keep your resume to one or two pages.
- **Proofreading**: Proofread your resume for spelling and grammar errors. Consider asking a friend or mentor to review it as well.

CRAFTING A COMPELLING COVER LETTER

1. Structure and Format
- **Header**: Include your contact information, the date, and the employer's contact information.
- **Salutation**: Address the letter to a specific person, if possible. Use "Dear [Hiring Manager's Name]" or "Dear Hiring Team" if the name is not available.
- **Introduction**: Start with a strong opening that captures the reader's attention. Mention the job you are applying for and briefly explain why you are interested in the position.
- **Body**: Highlight your relevant experience, skills, and accomplishments. You can use specific examples to show how you meet the job requirements.
- **Conclusion**: Summarize your qualifications and express your enthusiasm for the role. Include a call to action, such as requesting an interview. Thank the reader for their time and consideration.
- **Signature**: Sign off with a professional closing, such as "Sincerely" or "Best Regards," followed by your name.

www.lufsec.com

2. Customizing Your Cover Letter
- **Research the Company:** Mention specific details about the company and explain why you are excited to work there.
- **Align with Job Requirements**: Address the key requirements listed in the job description and explain how your background aligns with them.
- **Show Enthusiasm:** Convey your passion for cyber security and your eagerness to contribute to the organization's success.

3. Proofreading and Editing
- **Clarity and Conciseness**: Ensure your cover letter is clear, concise, and free of jargon. Aim for a length of one page.
- **Proofreading**: Carefully proofread your cover letter for spelling and grammar errors. Ask a friend or mentor to review it as well.

JOB SEARCH STRATEGIES

1. Networking
- Professional Associations: Join organizations like ISACA, ISC2, and local cyber security groups to connect with industry professionals.
- **Online Communitie**s: Participate in online forums and LinkedIn groups related to cyber security. You can engage in talks and share your expertise.
- **Conferences and Meetups**: Attend industry conferences, workshops, and meetups to expand your network and learn about job opportunities.

www.lufsec.com

2. Online Job Boards
- **General Job Boards:** Use platforms like LinkedIn, Indeed, and Glassdoor to search for cyber security jobs.
- **Specialized Job Boards**: Explore cyber security-specific job boards, such as CyberSecJobs, InfoSec Jobs, and ClearedJobs.net.

3. Company Websites
- **Direct Applications**: Visit the careers pages of companies you are interested in and apply directly to job postings.
- **Talent Pools**: Many companies allow you to join their talent pool or set up job alerts for future openings.

4. Recruiters and Staffing Agencies
- **Cyber Security Recruiters**: Work with recruiters who specialize in cyber security to access job opportunities that may not be publicly advertised.
- **Staffing Agencies**: Consider using staffing agencies that focus on IT and cyber security placements.

PREPARING FOR INTERVIEWS

1. Research the Company
- **Company Background**: Learn about the company's mission, values, products, services, and recent news.
- **Role and Responsibilities**: Understand the specific responsibilities and requirements of the job you are applying for.

www.lufsec.com

2. Common Interview Questions
- **Technical Questions:** Be prepared to answer questions about your technical skills, such as network security, penetration testing, and incident response.
- **Behavioral Questions**: Practice responding to behavioral questions using the STAR method (Situation, Task, Action, Result).
- **Problem-Solving Scenarios**: Be ready to discuss how you would handle specific security incidents or challenges.

3. Technical Assessments
- **Practical Tests:** You may be asked to complete practical tests or challenges to demonstrate your technical skills.
- **Certifications and Projects**: Be prepared to discuss any certifications, projects, or hands-on experience you have.

4. Questions to Ask the Interviewer
- **Role and Team**: Ask about the specific responsibilities of the role, the team you will be working with, and the company's approach to cyber security.
- **Professional Development**: Inquire about opportunities for training, certifications, and career advancement within the company.
- **Company Culture**: Ask about the company's culture, values, and work environment.

www.lufsec.com

Conclusion

The job search and application process can be challenging, but with the right strategies and preparation, you can enhance your chances of landing your desired role in cyber security. By building an effective resume, crafting a compelling cover letter, and preparing thoroughly for interviews, you can showcase your skills and qualifications to potential employers. In the next chapter, we will explore strategies for career advancement, including continuing education, networking, and professional development.

CHAPTER 9: CAREER ADVANCEMENT

Once you've established yourself in the field of cyber security, it's important to continuously seek opportunities for career advancement. This chapter explores various strategies for advancing your career, including continuing education, networking, professional development, and staying updated with industry trends.

CONTINUING EDUCATION AND ADVANCED CERTIFICATIONS

1. Pursuing Advanced Degrees

- **Master's Degree:** Consider pursuing a master's degree in cyber security or a related field to deepen your knowledge and open doors to senior-level positions.
- **Ph.D.:** For those interested in research and academia, a Ph.D. in cyber security can lead to opportunities in teaching and advanced research.

www.lufsec.com

2. Obtaining Advanced Certifications
- **Certified Information Systems Security Professional (CISSP):** An advanced certification for experienced professionals covering a broad range of security topics.
- **Certified Information Security Manager (CISM)**: Focuses on management and governance of information security programs.
- **Certified Information Systems Auditor (CISA)**: Emphasizes auditing, control, and assurance.
- **Offensive Security Certified Professional (OSCP)**: A hands-on certification for penetration testers.

3. Specialized Training Programs
- **SANS Institute**: Offers advanced courses and certifications in various cyber security domains.
- **GIAC Certifications**: Provides specialized certifications in areas like digital forensics, penetration testing, and incident handling.

NETWORKING AND PROFESSIONAL ASSOCIATIONS

1. Joining Professional Associations
- **ISACA**: An international professional association focused on IT governance, risk management, and security.
- **ISC2**: Offers certifications like CISSP and provides networking opportunities through local chapters.
- **SANS Institute**: Hosts events, conferences, and training programs for cyber security professionals.

www.lufsec.com

2. Attending Conferences and Events
- **Black Hat:** One of the largest and most prestigious information security conferences, offering training and networking opportunities.
- **DEF CON**: An annual hacker convention that provides a platform for learning and networking with other security professionals.
- **RSA Conference**: A major conference focused on security trends, research, and innovation.

3. Online Communities and Forums
- **Reddit (r/netsec)**: A community for discussing information security news and topics.
- **Stack Exchange (Information Security)**: A Q&A site for security professionals and enthusiasts.
- **LinkedIn Groups**: Join cybersecurity-related groups to connect with peers and share knowledge.

MENTORSHIP AND PROFESSIONAL DEVELOPMENT

1. Finding a Mentor
- **Industry Professionals**: Seek out experienced professionals who can provide guidance and advice.
- **Mentorship Programs**: Join formal mentorship programs offered by professional associations or your employer.
- **Luciano Ferrari at LufSec.com**: Luciano offers mentoring and coaching services, providing personalized guidance to help you advance in your cyber security career.

www.lufsec.com

2. **Providing Mentorship**
- **Giving Back:** As you gain experience, consider mentoring junior professionals to share your knowledge and expertise.
- **Developing Leadership Skills**: Mentoring others can help you develop valuable leadership and communication skills.

3. **Continuing Professional Development**
- **Workshops and Webinars**: Participate in workshops and webinars to stay updated on the latest security trends and technologies.
- **Professional Development Courses**: Enroll in courses that focus on leadership, project management, and other soft skills.

STAYING UPDATED WITH INDUSTRY TRENDS

1. **Following Industry News**
- **Cyber Security News Websites**: For the latest news and updates, regularly visit websites like Krebs on Security, The Hacker News, and Dark Reading.
- **Industry Blogs**: Follow blogs by security experts and organizations to stay informed about emerging threats and best practices.

2. **Engaging with Thought Leaders**
- **Social Media**: Follow industry thought leaders on platforms like Twitter and LinkedIn to gain insights and stay informed about the latest developments.
- **Podcasts and Webinars**: Listen to cyber security podcasts and attend webinars hosted by experts in the field.

www.lufsec.com

3. Participating in Research and Development
- **Open Source Projects:** Contribute to open source security projects to gain experience and collaborate with other professionals.
- **Publishing Research**: Write articles, whitepapers, or research papers on topics you are passionate about and share them with the community.

CAREER ADVANCEMENT STRATEGIES

1. Setting Career Goals
- **Short-Term Goals**: Identify immediate goals, such as obtaining a certification or completing a specific project.
- **Long-Term Goals**: Define your long-term career objectives, such as moving into a leadership role or specializing in a particular area of cyber security.

2. Seeking Promotions and New Opportunities
- **Internal Promotions**: Express your interest in taking on more responsibilities and seek opportunities for advancement within your current organization.
- **External Opportunities**: Stay open to job opportunities at other organizations that offer career growth and development.

3. Building a Personal Brand
- **Online Presence**: Maintain an updated LinkedIn profile and engage with the cyber security community through social media.

- **Public Speaking:** Volunteer to speak at conferences, webinars, or local meetups to share your expertise and build your reputation.

Conclusion

Advancing your career in cyber security requires a commitment to continuous learning, professional development, and networking. By pursuing advanced education and certifications, engaging with the professional community, and staying updated with industry trends, you can achieve your career goals and become a leader in the field. Remember, Luciano Ferrari at LufSec.com offers mentoring and coaching services, as well as certification study guides in the format of online courses and exam preparation/simulation, to help you on your journey.

www.lufsec.com

CHAPTER 10: RESOURCES AND TOOLS

Having the right resources and tools at your disposal is essential for success in the field of cyber security. This chapter provides a comprehensive list of recommended books, websites, online courses, tools, and communities that can help you stay informed, enhance your skills, and connect with other professionals.

RECOMMENDED BOOKS

1. **"The Web Application Hacker's Handbook"** by Dafydd Stuttard and Marcus Pinto
   - A comprehensive guide to web application security covering various attack vectors and defense mechanisms.

2. **"Hacking: The Art of Exploitation"** by Jon Erickson
   - A deep dive into hacking techniques and methodologies, providing practical examples and exercises.

www.lufsec.com

3. **"Metasploit: The Penetration Tester's Guide"** by David Kennedy, Jim O'Gorman, Devon Kearns, and Mati Aharoni
   - A detailed guide to using the Metasploit framework for penetration testing.

4. **"Applied Cryptography"** by Bruce Schneier
   - An authoritative book on cryptographic techniques and protocols.

5. **"Practical Malware Analysis"** by Michael Sikorski and Andrew Honig
   - A hands-on guide to analyzing and understanding malware.

RECOMMENDED WEBSITES

1. **Krebs on Security**
   - A leading blog by security expert Brian Krebs, covering the latest news and insights in cyber security.

2. **The Hacker News**
   - An online publication providing updates on the latest threats, vulnerabilities, and cyber security trends.

3. **Dark Reading**
   - A comprehensive source for news, analysis, and research on information security.

www.lufsec.com

4. OWASP (Open Web Application Security Project)
- A non-profit organization focused on improving the security of software, offering a wealth of resources and tools.

5. SANS Institute
- Provides a wide range of resources, including research, training, and certification programs.

RECOMMENDED ONLINE COURSES

1. LufSec.com
- Offers a variety of cyber security courses and training programs designed to equip you with practical, hands-on skills. Includes certification study guides and exam preparation/simulation.

2. Coursera
- It features courses and specializations in cybersecurity from top universities and organizations, such as the University of London and IBM.

3. edX
- It provides courses from institutions like Harvard University and MIT that cover various cybersecurity topics.

4. Udemy
- It features a wide range of cybersecurity courses, including ethical hacking, penetration testing, and more.

www.lufsec.com

4. OWASP (Open Web Application Security Project)
- A non-profit organization focused on improving the security of software, offering a wealth of resources and tools.

5. SANS Institute
- Provides a wide range of resources, including research, training, and certification programs.

RECOMMENDED ONLINE COURSES

1. LufSec.com
- Offers a variety of cyber security courses and training programs designed to equip you with practical, hands-on skills. Includes certification study guides and exam preparation/simulation.

2. Coursera
- It features courses and specializations in cybersecurity from top universities and organizations, such as the University of London and IBM.

3. edX
- It provides courses from institutions like Harvard University and MIT that cover various cybersecurity topics.

4. Udemy
- It features a wide range of cybersecurity courses, including ethical hacking, penetration testing, and more.

www.lufsec.com

5. **Cybrary**
   - A platform dedicated to cyber security training with courses for all skill levels.

ESSENTIAL TOOLS FOR CYBER SECURITY PROFESSIONALS

1. Network Scanners
- **Nmap**: A powerful network scanning tool for discovering hosts and services on a network.
- **Wireshark**: A network protocol analyzer for monitoring and troubleshooting network traffic.

2. Penetration Testing Tools
- **Metasploit**: A comprehensive framework for developing, testing, and executing exploits.
- **Burp Suite**: An integrated platform for performing security testing of web applications.
- **John the Ripper**: A fast password cracker for identifying weak passwords.

3. Malware Analysis Tools
- **IDA Pro**: A powerful disassembler for analyzing binary code.
- **OllyDbg**: An assembly-level debugger for analyzing and modifying binary code.
- **Cuckoo Sandbox**: An automated malware analysis system.

4. SIEM (Security Information and Event Management) Tools
- **Splunk:** A platform for searching, monitoring, and analyzing machine-generated data.
- **QRadar**: An IBM security intelligence platform for detecting and responding to threats.

5. Endpoint Protection Tools
- **Symantec Endpoint Protection**: A comprehensive solution for protecting endpoints from threats.
- **CrowdStrike Falcon**: A cloud-delivered endpoint protection platform for detecting and preventing threats.

ONLINE COMMUNITIES AND FORUMS

1. Reddit (r/netsec)
- A community for discussing information security news and topics.

2. Stack Exchange (Information Security)
- A Q&A site for security professionals and enthusiasts.

3. LinkedIn Groups
- Join cybersecurity-related groups to connect with peers and share knowledge.

4. Hack The Box
- An online platform for practicing penetration testing and cyber security challenges.

www.lufsec.com

5. **TryHackMe**
   - A platform offering hands-on labs and challenges to learn and practice cybersecurity skills.

PROFESSIONAL ASSOCIATIONS AND ORGANIZATIONS

1. **ISACA**
   - An international professional association focused on IT governance, risk management, and security.

2. **ISC2**
   - Offers certifications like CISSP and provides networking opportunities through local chapters.

3. **SANS Institute**
   - Hosts events, conferences, and training programs for cyber security professionals.

4. **OWASP**
   - A non-profit organization focused on improving the security of software, offering a wealth of resources and tools.

5. **ISSA (Information Systems Security Association)**
   - A global organization for information security professionals, providing resources, events, and networking opportunities.

www.lufsec.com

Conclusion

Access to the right resources and tools is crucial for continuous learning and professional growth in cyber security. By leveraging the recommended books, websites, online courses, tools, and communities mentioned in this chapter, you can enhance your skills, stay informed about the latest trends, and connect with other professionals.

This concludes the comprehensive guide on starting and advancing your cyber security career. By following the advice and strategies provided in this guide, you can build a successful and fulfilling career in this dynamic and rapidly evolving field.

---

www.lufsec.com

Printed in Great Britain
by Amazon